Mastering Marketing for Small Businesses:

Your Comprehensive Guide For Marketing Success

20
23

I0431811

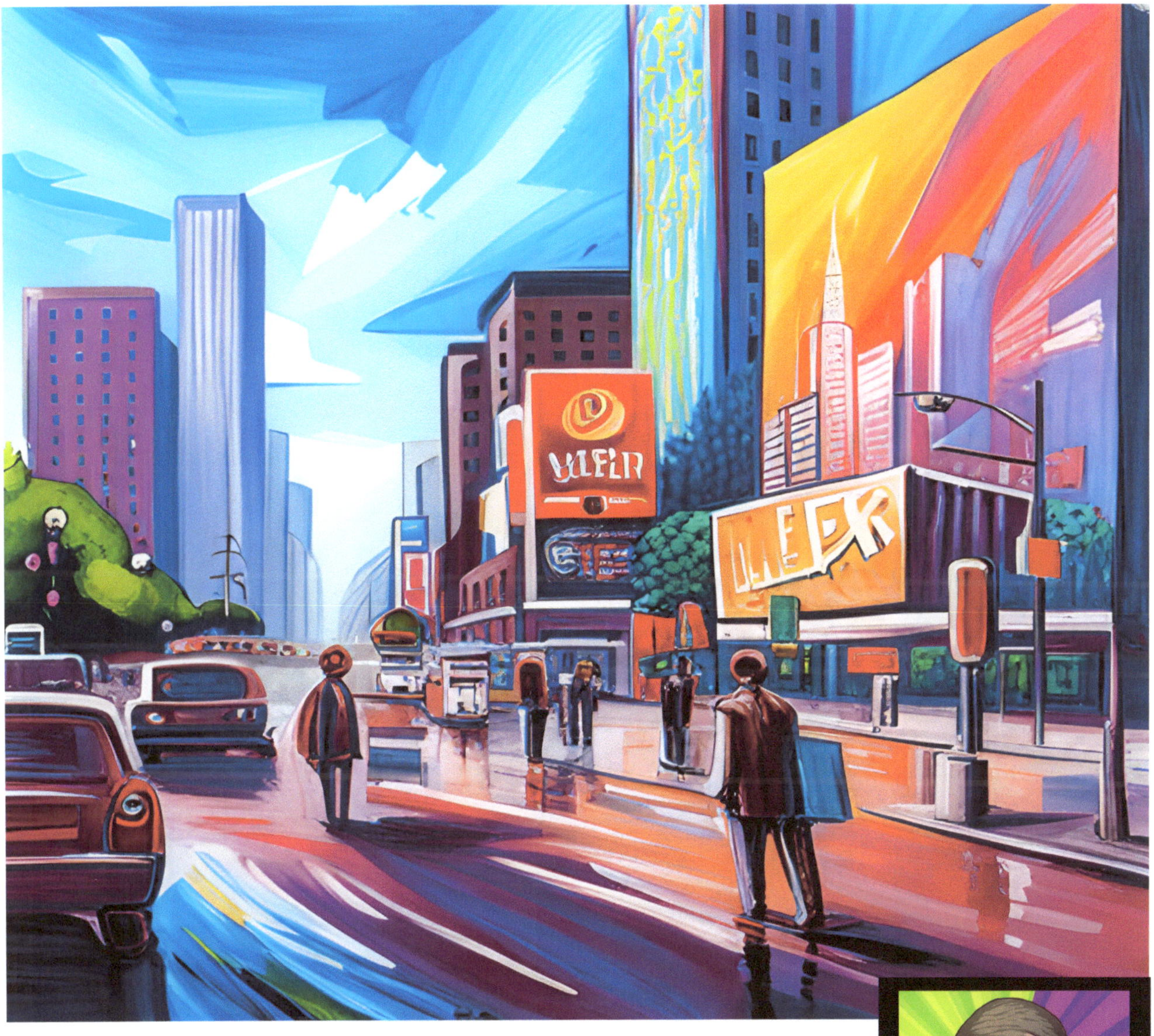

WRITTEN AND ILLUSTRATED BY

Keith Hanshaw

TABLE OF CONTENT

1. Introduction to Advertising and Marketing for Small Business Owners
2. Defining Your Target Audience and Market Segmentation
3. Building Your Brand Identity: Logo, Messaging, and Visual Elements
4. Crafting a Unique Value Proposition and Brand Identity
5. The Power of Radio Advertising: Cumulus Media Research Insights
6. Harnessing the Reach of Local TV and Cable Advertising
7. Print Advertising: Newspapers, Magazines, and Direct Mail
8. Outdoor Advertising: Billboards, Transit, and Street Furniture
9. Digital Marketing Essentials: Websites, Social Media, and Email Marketing
10. Search Engine Optimization (SEO) and Pay-Per-Click (PPC) Advertising
11. Content Marketing: Blogging, Podcasting, and Video Production
12. Influencer Marketing: Leveraging Social Media Personalities
13. Event Marketing: Trade Shows, Expos, and Community Events
14. Sponsorships and Partnerships: Collaborating for Success
15. Measuring Your Marketing Success: Analytics and Key Performance Indicators (KPIs)
16. Creating an Integrated Marketing Plan: Combining Traditional and Digital Strategies
17. Growth Hacking Techniques for Small Businesses
18. The Future of Advertising and Marketing: Trends to Watch
19. Case Studies of Successful Small Business Marketing Campaigns
20. Final Thoughts

Chapter 1

Chapter 1:
Introduction to Advertising and Marketing for Small Business Owners

Welcome to the world of advertising and marketing for small business owners! This book is designed to provide you with a comprehensive understanding of advertising strategies, backed by research, experience, and real-world case studies. My primary goal is to help you become the business or brand that customers think of first (and feel best about) when a triggering event in their life creates a need or want for the product or service your company provides.

To begin, let's discuss why businesses advertise and why customers buy things.

We buy things for two reasons: we need them, or we want them.

These needs and wants are often created by triggering events, which happen every day. For example, someone might get a flat tire, prompting them to call a tow truck or visit a tire shop. **The decision to buy takes place in our minds**, not online or in a store. **That's why it's crucial to be "known before you're needed or wanted."**

Being known is especially important because 80% of people are likely or very likely to shop at the first place that comes to mind.

The FOUR Keys of Advertising Success

REACH

4 Keys to Successful advertising

To become known, there are four keys to successful advertising:

1. **Reach**:
You need to reach a wide audience of potential customers.

2. **Frequency**:
Your target audience must hear or see your message frequently.

3. **Consistency**:
Maintain a consistent advertising presence, as people are always in different buying cycles.

4. **Message**:
Craft a compelling message that resonates with your audience.

8 Characteristics of successful advertising

Now, let's examine the common characteristics of the best-performing advertising, which can help you decide which local media options will work best for your business:

1. Reach your potential customers
2. Influence them close to the point of purchase
3. Provide local consumer interactions
4. Create emotional connections
5. Build trust & credibility
6. Provide un-skippable engagement
7. Be cost-effective
8. Deliver affordable ads quickly

With several local advertising options available, such as TV, cable, newspapers, digital, radio, outdoor, and direct mail, choosing the right mix can be overwhelming. However, by focusing on these characteristics and the four keys to successful advertising, you'll be better equipped to create effective marketing campaigns that drive results for your small business.

Throughout this book, we will delve into various marketing principles and tips designed to help new small business owners succeed in their advertising efforts. We will also feature real-world case studies to demonstrate the effectiveness of these strategies.

In addition to the valuable information provided in this book, I invite you to listen to the **Small Biz Buzz** podcast, which offers further insights and advice on marketing for small business owners.

You're also encouraged to visit **FreeMarketingHelp.org** and request a free copy of my marketing guide specifically tailored for small business owners. While this book provides more detailed information, the free version is an excellent resource if you need to quickly grasp the basics and jump right into action. By following the guidance provided in this book and utilizing the additional resources mentioned, you'll be well-equipped to create successful marketing campaigns that drive results for your small business.

Chapter 2:
Defining Your Target Audience and Market Segmentation

To create effective advertising campaigns that resonate with potential customers and drive results for your small business, it's essential to define your target audience and segment your market. This chapter will guide you through the process of identifying your ideal customers and understanding their needs, preferences, and behaviors.

Defining Your Target Audience

Your target audience consists of the people who are most likely to be interested in your products or services. These individuals share common characteristics, such as demographics, geographic location, interests, and behavior patterns, which make them more receptive to your marketing messages.

To define your target audience, consider the following steps:

1. **Analyze your current customer base:** Identify the traits that your existing customers have in common, such as age, gender, income, location, and interests. This information will provide valuable insights into the types of people who are already attracted to your business.

2. **Identify your competitors' target audience:** Research your competitors and determine who they are targeting with their marketing efforts. Understanding their target audience can help you find gaps in the market or areas where you can differentiate your offerings.

3. **Consider your product or service:** Analyze the features and benefits of your products or services and identify the types of customers who would be most interested in them. This will help you create a profile of your ideal customer.

4. **Create customer personas:** Develop detailed profiles of your ideal customers, including demographic information, interests, preferences, and pain points. These personas can guide your marketing efforts and help you tailor your messaging to resonate with your target audience.

Market Segmentation

Once you've identified your target audience, it's important to segment your market to create more targeted and effective marketing campaigns. Market segmentation involves dividing your target audience into smaller groups based on shared characteristics.

Common types of market segmentation include:

1. **Demographic segmentation:** This involves dividing your market based on factors such as age, gender, income, education, and family size.

2. **Geographic segmentation:** This type of segmentation focuses on the location of your target audience, such as their country, region, city, or neighborhood.

3. **Psychographic segmentation:** This involves categorizing your audience based on their personality traits, interests, values, attitudes, and lifestyles.

4. **Behavioral segmentation:** This type of segmentation divides your market based on how customers interact with your products or services, including their purchase history, usage patterns, and brand loyalty.

By defining your target audience and segmenting your market, you can create more personalized and relevant advertising campaigns that resonate with potential customers and drive results for your small business. In the following chapters, we will discuss various marketing strategies and channels that can help you reach and engage your target audience effectively.

Chapter 3: Building Your Brand Identity: Logo, Messaging, and Visual Elements

A strong brand identity is essential for establishing your business in the minds of consumers and differentiating yourself from competitors. In this chapter, we'll discuss the importance of crafting a compelling brand identity, focusing on three key components: logo, messaging, and visual elements.

Logo Design

Your logo is often the first visual representation of your brand that customers encounter. A well-designed logo should be unique, memorable, and easily recognizable, reflecting your brand's personality and values.

Here are some tips to help you create an effective logo:

1. **Simplicity:** Keep your logo design simple and clean, making it easy to identify and recall.
2. **Scalability:** Ensure your logo is versatile and can be used across various sizes and formats without losing its impact or clarity.
3. **Color palette:** Choose colors that represent your brand's personality and evoke the right emotions in your target audience. Limit your color palette to maintain consistency and avoid clutter.
4. **Typography:** Select a font that complements your logo's design and reflects your brand's style. Avoid using too many different fonts, which can make your logo appear chaotic and unprofessional.

Messaging

Your brand messaging communicates your company's values, mission, and unique selling proposition (USP) to your target audience. It should be consistent across all marketing channels and resonate with your customers.

Consider these tips when developing your brand messaging:

1. **Define your USP:** Identify what sets your business apart from competitors and focus on the benefits your products or services provide.

2. **Speak to your target audience:** Use language and tone that appeal to your target market, addressing their needs, preferences, and pain points.

3. **Be consistent:** Ensure that your messaging remains consistent across all marketing materials and channels to build a cohesive brand image.

Visual Elements

Visual elements, such as color schemes, typography, and imagery, play a crucial role in creating a cohesive and memorable brand identity.

Here are some guidelines for developing your brand's visual elements:

1. Color scheme: Develop a consistent color palette that represents your brand and evokes the desired emotions in your target audience. Use these colors across all marketing materials and channels.

2. Typography: Choose fonts that align with your brand's personality and are easily readable. Maintain consistency by using the same fonts throughout your marketing materials.

3. Imagery: Select images and graphics that complement your brand identity and effectively comunite your messaging. Use high-quality visuals to create a professional appearance and leave a lasting impression on your audience. By focusing on these three components—logo, messaging, and visual elements—you can build a strong brand identity that resonates with your target market and sets usiness apart from competitors. In the next chapters, we'll explore various marketing strategies andchannels to help you effectively promote your brand and reach your target audience.

Chapter 4:
Crafting a Unique Value Proposition and Brand Identity

A unique value proposition (UVP) is a clear, concise statement that communicates the benefits your business offers and how it distinguishes itself from competitors. Your UVP plays a crucial role in shaping your brand identity and resonating with your target audience. In this chapter, we'll explore the steps to crafting a compelling UVP and integrating it into your overall brand identity.

Crafting a Unique Value Proposition

To create an effective UVP, follow these steps:

1. **Identify your target audience:** Clearly define your ideal customers, considering their demographics, preferences, and pain points. Your UVP should be tailored to address the specific needs of this audience.
2. **Analyze your competitors:** Study your competitors' offerings and identify areas where your products or services differ. Understanding your competition will help you emphasize your unique strengths in your UVP.
3. **List your key benefits:** Determine the main benefits your products or services provide to customers. Focus on the value these benefits offer, such as solving a problem, saving time, or improving quality of life.
4. **Highlight your differentiators:** Identify the aspects of your business that set you apart from competitors. These could include superior quality, exceptional customer service, innovative technology, or exclusive features.
5. **Create a concise statement:** Combine your key benefits and differentiators into a clear, concise statement that communicates your unique value.

Your UVP should be easy to understand and memorable.

Integrating Your UVP into Your Brand Identity

Once you've crafted your UVP, integrate it into your overall brand identity by incorporating it into your messaging, visual elements, and marketing strategies. Here are some tips for doing so:

1. **Incorporate your UVP into your messaging:** Ensure that your UVP is consistently communicated across all marketing channels, including your website, social media, advertising campaigns, and promotional materials.
2. **Design visual elements that reflect your UVP:** Create a cohesive brand identity by designing visual elements, such as your logo, color scheme, and imagery, that align with your UVP. These elements should effectively convey the unique value your business offers.
3. **Create content that supports your UVP:** Develop content, such as blog posts, case studies, and testimonials, that reinforces your UVP and demonstrates the benefits and differentiators of your products or services.
4. **Train your team to communicate your UVP:** Educate your employees on your UVP and ensure they can effectively communicate it to customers and prospects. Your team should be well-versed in the unique value your business provides and be able to articulate it clearly.

By crafting a compelling UVP and integrating it into your brand identity, you'll effectively communicate the unique value your business offers and create a strong connection with your target audience. In the following chapters, we'll explore various marketing strategies and channels to help you promote your brand and reach your target market effectively.

Chapter 5:
The Power of Radio Advertising: Cumulus Media Research Insights

Radio advertising remains a powerful and effective marketing tool for businesses, reaching a wide audience and offering unique advantages over other media options. In this chapter, we'll explore the benefits of radio advertising, supported by research insights from Cumulus Media, a leading audio-first media company. We'll also highlight the expertise of Pierre Bouvard, Cumulus Media and Westwood One's Chief Insights Officer, who has contributed extensively to the understanding of radio advertising's impact.

Benefits of Radio Advertising

Radio advertising offers several benefits that make it an attractive option for small businesses:

1. **Wide reach:** Radio reaches a diverse audience across various age groups, demographics, and locations, ensuring your message is heard by potential customers.

2. **Targeted advertising:** Radio allows you to target specific segments of your audience based on factors such as geographic location, listening habits, and preferred station formats.

3. **Cost-effective:** Compared to other advertising channels, radio offers affordable ad rates and production costs, delivering a high return on investment (ROI).

4. **Flexible and timely:** Radio ads can be produced and aired quickly, allowing you to respond to market changes or capitalize on current events and trends.

5. **Emotional connection:** Radio's storytelling format fosters an emotional connection with listeners, making your message more memorable and impactful.

Cumulus Media Research Insights

Cumulus Media's research, led by Pierre Bouvard, has revealed valuable insights into the effectiveness of radio advertising:

1. **High ROI:** Radio consistently delivers a high ROI, outperforming other local media options. According to Nielsen's ROI studies, every dollar spent on radio advertising generates an average of $12 in sales, with some campaigns achieving an ROI of up to $25.

2. **Increased brand awareness:** Radio advertising has been shown to significantly increase brand awareness, with campaigns resulting in a 29% lift in unaided brand recall.

3. **Influence on purchasing decisions:** Radio is effective at influencing consumers' purchasing decisions, especially when ads are aired close to the point of purchase. Research shows that radio advertising can increase store traffic by an average of 22% and online search activity by 29%.

4. **Synergy with other media channels:** Combining radio advertising with other media platforms, such as digital, can further increase ROI. Research indicates that adding radio to a media mix can boost overall campaign effectiveness by 20%.

Pierre Bouvard's insights and research emphasize the power of radio advertising in driving results for businesses. By leveraging radio's unique benefits and incorporating it into your marketing strategy, you can reach your target audience effectively and achieve a high ROI. In the following chapters, we'll explore additional marketing strategies and channels to help you create a comprehensive and successful advertising campaign for your small business.

Chapter 6: Harnessing the Reach of Local TV and Cable Advertising

Local TV and cable advertising offer businesses an effective way to reach a broad audience and create a strong visual impact. In this chapter, we'll discuss the benefits of local TV and cable advertising and provide tips for maximizing their potential in your marketing campaigns.

Benefits of Local TV and Cable Advertising

Local TV and cable advertising provide several advantages for businesses looking to promote their products or services:

1. **Wide reach:** Local TV and cable networks reach a large audience in specific geographic areas, allowing you to target potential customers in your community.

2. **Visual storytelling:** TV advertising enables you to showcase your products or services through compelling visual storytelling, which can create a lasting impression on viewers.

3. **Targeted advertising:** Cable advertising allows you to target specific demographics and interests by selecting channels and programming that cater to your desired audience.

4. **Credibility:** Local TV stations are often trusted sources of news and information, which can lend credibility to your brand when advertising on these platforms.

Tips for Effective Local TV and Cable Advertising

To maximize the effectiveness of your local TV and cable advertising campaigns, consider the following tips:

1. **Define your target audience:** Clearly identify your ideal customers and their preferences, ensuring your ads resonate with the viewers most likely to be interested in your products or services.

2. **Create high-quality content:** Invest in professional-quality video production to create engaging, visually appealing ads that reflect your brand's identity and convey your unique value proposition.

3. **Choose the right time slots:** Select time slots and programming that align with your target audience's habits and preferences, maximizing the chances of reaching potential customers when they're most receptive to your message.

4. **Track and measure results:** Monitor the performance of your TV and cable advertising campaigns using metrics such as reach, frequency, and audience engagement. Use this data to optimize your campaigns and maximize your return on investment (ROI).

5. **Integrate with other marketing channels:** Combine your TV and cable advertising efforts with other marketing channels, such as radio, digital, and social media, to create a cohesive and comprehensive marketing strategy.

By harnessing the reach of local TV and cable advertising and incorporating these tips into your marketing campaigns, you can effectively promote your brand, reach your target audience, and drive results for your small business. In the upcoming chapters, we'll explore additional marketing strategies and channels to help you create a well-rounded advertising campaign that achieves your business goals.

Chapter 7

Chapter 7:
Print Advertising: Newspapers, Magazines, and Direct Mail

Print advertising, which includes newspapers, magazines, and direct mail, has been a traditional method of reaching audiences for many years. However, it's important to note that while I'm sharing information on these formats, I personally believe that radio and digital display advertising can provide a more efficient and higher frequency way of targeting the same list of people.

Addressable geo-fencing allows you to target specific addresses and connect with internet-connected devices inside those homes. With digital display, you can reach your customers multiple times within a 30-day period or more, depending on your budget and marketing goals.

Newspapers and Magazines

Newspapers and magazines offer various benefits, such as local focus, credibility, targeted audience, high-quality visuals, and longer shelf life. However, these traditional advertising methods may not provide the same level of frequency and efficiency as digital display advertising.

Direct Mail

Direct mail involves sending promotional materials directly to potential customers via postal mail. While this method allows for personalization, targeted reach, and measurable results, it may not be as efficient or effective as digital display advertising in terms of frequency and engagement.

Digital Display Advertising

Digital display advertising, particularly addressable geo-fencing, offers several advantages over traditional print advertising:

1. **Higher frequency:** You can reach your target audience multiple times within a specified period, increasing the chances of your message being seen and remembered.

2. **Greater efficiency:** Digital display advertising allows you to target specific addresses with precision, ensuring that your ads are shown to the right people.

3. **Flexibility:** Digital campaigns can be adjusted quickly based on performance data, allowing you to optimize your ads for better results.

4. **Cost-effectiveness:** Digital display advertising can often provide a higher return on investment compared to traditional print advertising, as you can reach a larger audience with a smaller budget.

To maximize the effectiveness of your marketing campaigns, consider incorporating digital display advertising into your strategy alongside traditional print advertising methods.

This integrated approach can help you achieve your marketing goals more efficiently and effectively by harnessing the strengths of both traditional and digital advertising channels. In the next chapters, we'll continue exploring various marketing strategies and channels to help you create well-rounded advertising campaigns that achieve your business goals.

Chapter 8

Chapter 8: Outdoor Advertising: Billboards, Transit, and Street Furniture

Outdoor advertising, also known as out-of-home (OOH) advertising, is a powerful way to reach potential customers as they go about their daily lives. This type of advertising encompasses a variety of formats, including billboards, transit, and street furniture. In this chapter, we'll discuss the benefits of each format and provide tips for creating successful outdoor advertising campaigns.

Billboards

Billboards are large, eye-catching displays placed along highways, busy streets, or other high-traffic areas. Benefits of billboard advertising include:

1. **High visibility:** Billboards are designed to be seen by large numbers of people, making them an effective way to raise brand awareness.

2. **Strategic placement:** Billboards can be strategically placed in prime locations to target specific demographics or geographic areas.

3. **Long-term exposure:** Unlike some other forms of advertising, billboards offer extended periods of exposure, increasing the chances of your message being seen and remembered.

Transit Advertising

Transit advertising involves placing ads on buses, trains, taxis, or other public transportation vehicles, as well as in transit stations. Benefits of transit advertising include:

1. **Wide reach:** Transit ads can reach a diverse audience of commuters and travelers, ensuring your message is seen by many potential customers.

2. **Repeated exposure:** As people use public transportation regularly, they are likely to see your ad multiple times, reinforcing your message.

3. **Localized targeting:** Transit ads can be placed on specific routes or in specific areas, allowing you to target your desired audience more effectively.

Street Furniture Advertising

Street furniture advertising refers to ads placed on items such as bus shelters, benches, kiosks, and phone booths. Benefits of street furniture advertising include:

1. **High foot traffic:** Street furniture ads are typically placed in busy urban areas, ensuring visibility among pedestrians and motorists.

2. **Localized targeting:** Similar to transit advertising, street furniture ads can be placed in specific neighborhoods or areas to reach your target audience.

3. **Community engagement:** Street furniture ads can contribute to the aesthetics of a community while also providing useful amenities, such as seating or shelter.

Tips for Effective Outdoor Advertising Campaigns

To create successful outdoor advertising campaigns, consider the following tips:

1. **Keep it simple:** Outdoor ads should be easy to understand at a glance. Use concise messaging and bold visuals to quickly communicate your message.

2. **Be strategic with location:** Choose locations that provide the most visibility and relevance to your target audience.

3. **Use eye-catching design:** Create visually appealing ads that stand out and capture the attention of passersby.

4. **Integrate with other marketing channels:** Combine your outdoor advertising efforts with other marketing channels, such as digital, radio, and TV, to create a cohesive and comprehensive marketing strategy.

By leveraging the benefits of billboards, transit, and street furniture advertising, and incorporating these tips into your campaigns, you can effectively promote your brand, reach your target audience, and drive results for your small business. In the following chapters, we'll explore more marketing strategies and channels to help you create well-rounded advertising campaigns that achieve your business goals.

Chapter 9:
Digital Marketing Essentials: Websites, Social Media, and Email Marketing

Digital marketing has become an essential component of a successful marketing strategy for businesses of all sizes. In this chapter, we'll discuss the importance of having a strong online presence through websites, social media, and email marketing and provide tips for effectively utilizing these channels.

Websites

A professional, user-friendly website is crucial for any business looking to establish credibility and attract potential customers. Key elements of an effective website include:

1. **Responsive design:** Ensure your website is mobile-friendly and adapts to different screen sizes and devices.

2. **Clear navigation:** Make it easy for visitors to find the information they're looking for with a well-organized menu and intuitive layout.

3. **Compelling content:** Provide valuable content that showcases your products or services, addresses customer pain points, and highlights your unique value proposition.

4. **Search engine optimization (SEO):** Optimize your website for search engines to improve its visibility and attract more organic traffic.

Social Media

Social media platforms offer an excellent opportunity to engage with your target audience, build brand awareness, and showcase your products or services. To make the most of social media marketing, consider the following tips:

1. **Choose the right platforms:** Focus on the social media platforms where your target audience is most active and engaged.

2. **Create engaging content:** Share a mix of promotional, educational, and entertaining content that resonates with your audience.

3. **Consistency:** Maintain a consistent posting schedule to keep your audience engaged and foster brand recognition.

4. **Interact with your audience:** Respond to comments, messages, and mentions to build relationships with your followers and demonstrate excellent customer service.

Email Marketing

Email marketing is a cost-effective way to communicate directly with your target audience, promote your products or services, and nurture customer relationships. Tips for successful email marketing campaigns include:

1. **Build a quality email list:** Collect email addresses from interested prospects through website sign-up forms, in-store promotions, or social media campaigns.

2. **Segment your list:** Divide your email list into segments based on factors such as demographics, purchasing behavior, or engagement to create more targeted and relevant campaigns.

3. **Craft compelling content:** Write engaging subject lines and email copy that provide value to your subscribers and encourage them to take action.

4. **Measure and optimize:** Track key performance metrics, such as open rates, click-through rates, and conversions, to identify areas for improvement and optimize future campaigns.

By incorporating website development, social media marketing, and email marketing into your digital marketing strategy, you can effectively reach and engage with your target audience, driving results for your small business. In the next chapters, we'll explore additional marketing strategies and channels to help you create a comprehensive and successful advertising campaign that achieves your business goals.

Chapter 10:
Search Engine Optimization (SEO) and Pay-Per-Click (PPC) Advertising

Both Search Engine Optimization (SEO) and Pay-Per-Click (PPC) advertising play crucial roles in driving traffic to your website and increasing online visibility. In this chapter, we'll discuss the differences between SEO and PPC, their benefits, and tips for effectively utilizing these digital marketing strategies.

Search Engine Optimization (SEO)

SEO is the process of improving your website's visibility on search engines like Google, Bing, and Yahoo. By optimizing your site's content, structure, and performance, you can achieve higher organic rankings and attract more traffic. Key aspects of SEO include:

1. **Keyword research:** Identify relevant keywords that your target audience uses when searching for products or services similar to yours.

2. **On-page optimization:** Optimize your website's content, meta tags, headings, and images to align with your target keywords.

3. **Technical SEO:** Improve your site's performance, mobile-friendliness, and overall user experience to meet search engine guidelines.

4. **Link building:** Acquire high-quality backlinks from reputable sites to increase your website's authority and improve its search engine rankings.

Pay-Per-Click (PPC) Advertising

PPC advertising involves placing online ads that only charge you when someone clicks on them. Google Ads is the most popular PPC platform, allowing you to bid on specific keywords and display your ads at the top of search engine results pages (SERPs). Benefits of PPC advertising include:

1. **Immediate visibility:** PPC ads can provide instant exposure on search engines, making them an effective way to generate traffic quickly.

2. **Targeted reach:** PPC allows you to target specific keywords, demographics, locations, and devices, ensuring your ads reach the right audience.

3. **Budget control:** You can set a daily budget and maximum bid for your ads, giving you full control over your advertising costs.

4. **Measurable results:** PPC platforms provide detailed analytics, allowing you to track your campaign's performance and ROI.

Tips for Effective SEO and PPC Strategies

To maximize the effectiveness of your SEO and PPC efforts, consider the following tips:

1. **Align your SEO and PPC strategies:** Use insights from your PPC campaigns to inform your SEO efforts and vice versa. This can help you identify high-performing keywords and ad copy that can be used for both strategies.

2. **Perform regular keyword research:** Stay up-to-date with keyword trends and adjust your SEO and PPC campaigns accordingly to maintain relevance and competitiveness.

3. **Optimize landing pages:** Ensure your PPC ads direct users to relevant, optimized landing pages that provide a seamless user experience and encourage conversions.

4. **Monitor and adjust:** Regularly analyze your SEO and PPC performance data to identify areas for improvement and make adjustments as needed.

By effectively implementing SEO and PPC strategies, you can increase your online visibility, drive targeted traffic to your website, and boost conversions for your small business. In the following chapters, we'll explore more marketing strategies and channels to help you create well-rounded advertising campaigns that achieve your business goals.

Chapter 11: Content Marketing: Blogging, Podcasting, and Video Production

Content marketing is a strategic approach that involves creating, distributing, and promoting valuable, relevant, and consistent content to attract and engage a target audience. In this chapter, we'll discuss three popular content marketing formats – blogging, podcasting, and video production – and provide tips for effectively utilizing these channels.

Blogging

Blogging is a powerful way to share your expertise, educate your audience, and establish yourself as an industry thought leader. Benefits of blogging include:

1. **Increased website traffic:** Regularly posting high-quality blog content can help improve your website's search engine rankings and attract more organic traffic.

2. **Lead generation:** Offering valuable content can encourage visitors to subscribe to your email list or request more information about your products or services.

3. **Brand authority:** Providing informative and engaging content can help position your brand as an expert in your industry.

Podcasting

Podcasting allows you to create audio content that can be easily consumed by your target audience while they're commuting, working out, or completing other tasks. Benefits of podcasting include:

1. **Personal connection:** Podcasts enable you to connect with your audience on a personal level, fostering trust and loyalty.

2. **Niche targeting:** Podcasts can cater to specific interests or industries, allowing you to reach a highly engaged audience.

3. **Ease of production:** Podcasts generally require less production effort and equipment compared to video content, making them more accessible for small businesses.

Video Production

Video content is highly engaging and can help you effectively communicate complex ideas, showcase your products or services, and tell your brand story. Benefits of video production include:

1. **High engagement:** Videos are more likely to be shared and have higher retention rates compared to text-based content.

2. **Versatility:** Video content can be used across various platforms, such as your website, social media channels, or email campaigns.

3. **Increased conversions:** Compelling video content can help drive leads and conversions by showcasing the value of your products or services.

Tips for Effective Content Marketing

To maximize the effectiveness of your content marketing efforts, consider the following tips:

1. **Know your audience:** Understand your target audience's needs, preferences, and pain points to create content that resonates with them.

2. **Create a content calendar:** Plan and schedule your content production and promotion to ensure consistency and relevancy.

3. **Optimize for SEO:** Incorporate relevant keywords into your content to improve its search engine visibility and attract more organic traffic.

4. **Promote your content:** Share your content across various marketing channels, such as social media, email, or paid advertising, to increase its reach and visibility.

By leveraging blogging, podcasting, and video production in your content marketing strategy, you can effectively engage your target audience, showcase your expertise, and drive results for your small business. In the following chapters, we'll explore additional marketing strategies and channels to help you create well-rounded advertising campaigns that achieve your business goals.

BRAND EARLY, BRAND OFTEN!

Chapter 12: Influencer Marketing: Leveraging Social Media Personalities

Influencer marketing is a strategy that involves partnering with influential individuals, often on social media platforms, to promote your brand, products, or services. These influencers have established credibility and a loyal following within their niche, making them valuable partners for businesses looking to reach a specific audience. In this chapter, we'll discuss the benefits of influencer marketing and provide tips for effectively utilizing this marketing channel.

Benefits of Influencer Marketing

1. **Trust and credibility:** Influencers have already built trust with their followers, so their recommendations can carry more weight than traditional advertising methods.

2. **Targeted reach:** Influencers typically have a specific niche, allowing you to reach a highly engaged and relevant audience.

3. **High engagement:** Influencer content tends to generate higher engagement rates compared to traditional advertising, leading to increased brand awareness and potential conversions.

4. **Cost-effective:** Depending on the influencer, partnerships can be more cost-effective than other marketing channels, especially when targeting a niche audience.

Tips for Effective Influencer Marketing

To maximize the effectiveness of your influencer marketing efforts, consider the following tips:

1. **Choose the right influencers:** Look for influencers whose audience aligns with your target market and who share values and interests relevant to your brand.

2. **Evaluate their engagement:** Focus on influencers with high engagement rates, as this indicates a strong connection with their followers and a higher likelihood of generating results.

3. **Establish clear goals:** Define your objectives for the partnership, such as increasing brand awareness, driving website traffic, or boosting sales. Communicate these goals with the influencer to ensure alignment.

4. **Develop a mutually beneficial relationship:** Collaborate with the influencer on content ideas and provide them with creative freedom while ensuring the partnership aligns with your brand identity and goals.

5. **Track and measure results:** Monitor the performance of your influencer marketing campaigns, including engagement, conversions, and ROI. Use this data to optimize future partnerships and strategies.

By leveraging influencer marketing, you can tap into the power of social media personalities to reach a highly engaged and targeted audience, increasing brand awareness and driving results for your small business. In the following chapters, we'll explore more marketing strategies and channels to help you create well-rounded advertising campaigns that achieve your business goals.

Chapter 13: Event Marketing: Trade Shows, Expos, and Community Events

Event marketing is a strategic approach that involves promoting your brand, products, or services through in-person or virtual events such as trade shows, expos, and community events. In this chapter, we'll discuss the benefits of event marketing and provide tips for effectively utilizing this marketing channel.

Benefits of Event Marketing

1. **Face-to-face interaction:** Events provide an opportunity for direct engagement with potential customers, allowing you to build relationships and showcase your products or services.

2. **Targeted audience:** Trade shows and expos often attract attendees who are already interested in your industry or niche, ensuring a relevant audience for your marketing efforts.

3. **Brand exposure:** Participating in events can help increase brand awareness and visibility, both among attendees and within your industry.

4. **Networking opportunities:** Events offer the chance to connect with other industry professionals and potential partners, fostering collaboration and growth.

Tips for Effective Event Marketing

To maximize the effectiveness of your event marketing efforts, consider the following tips:

1. **Set clear objectives:** Define your goals for participating in the event, such as generating leads, increasing brand awareness, or launching a new product. This will help guide your planning and promotional efforts.

2. **Choose the right events:** Research and select events that align with your target audience, industry, and marketing objectives.

3. **Create an engaging booth or exhibit:** Design a visually appealing and interactive space that attracts attendees and encourages them to engage with your brand.

4. **Promote your presence:** Utilize your website, social media channels, and email marketing to inform your audience about your participation in the event and any special promotions or activities you have planned.

5. **Train your event staff:** Ensure your team is well-prepared to represent your brand and engage with attendees, providing them with the necessary information and resources.

6. **Follow up with leads:** After the event, promptly follow up with any leads or contacts you've collected to nurture relationships and encourage conversions.

By leveraging event marketing, you can create memorable experiences for your target audience, increase brand exposure, and drive results for your small business. In the following chapters, we'll explore more marketing strategies and channels to help you create well-rounded advertising campaigns that achieve your business goals.

Chapter 14: Sponsorships and Partnerships: Collaborating for Success

Sponsorships and partnerships involve collaborating with other businesses, organizations, or individuals to achieve mutual marketing objectives. In this chapter, we'll discuss the benefits of sponsorships and partnerships and provide tips for effectively utilizing these marketing channels.

Benefits of Sponsorships and Partnerships

1. **Increased brand exposure:** Collaborating with another organization or individual can expose your brand to a new audience, expanding your reach and visibility.
2. **Shared resources:** Partnerships can help you access additional resources, such as marketing budgets, expertise, or distribution channels, that might be otherwise unavailable to you.
3. **Enhanced credibility:** Associating your brand with a well-respected partner can boost your credibility and trustworthiness in the eyes of potential customers.
4. **Cost-effective marketing:** By pooling resources and sharing marketing efforts, sponsorships and partnerships can often be more cost-effective than traditional advertising methods.

Tips for Effective Sponsorships and Partnerships

To maximize the effectiveness of your sponsorships and partnerships, consider the following tips:

1. **Choose the right partners:** Look for partners whose target audience, values, and objectives align with your own. This will ensure a more successful and mutually beneficial collaboration.

2. **Define clear goals:** Establish clear objectives for the partnership, such as increasing brand awareness, reaching a new market segment, or launching a joint product or service.

3. **Develop a collaborative marketing plan:** Work together with your partner to create a comprehensive marketing plan that leverages both parties' strengths and resources.

4. **Communicate regularly:** Maintain open communication with your partner to ensure alignment, address any challenges, and adapt strategies as needed.

5. **Measure and evaluate success:** Track the performance of your partnership through key performance indicators (KPIs), such as leads generated, sales, or brand exposure. Use this data to optimize your collaboration and inform future partnerships.

By leveraging sponsorships and partnerships, you can tap into new audiences, resources, and opportunities, creating a win-win situation for both parties and driving results for your small business. In the following chapters, we'll explore more marketing strategies and channels to help you create well-rounded advertising campaigns that achieve your business goals.

Chapter 15

Chapter 15: Measuring Your Marketing Success: Analytics and Key Performance Indicators (KPIs)

Effectively measuring the success of your marketing efforts is crucial for making informed decisions, optimizing strategies, and maximizing ROI. In this chapter, we'll discuss the importance of analytics and key performance indicators (KPIs) in evaluating your marketing success.

Importance of Analytics and KPIs

1. **Data-driven decision-making:** Analytics and KPIs provide valuable insights into the performance of your marketing campaigns, allowing you to make data-driven decisions and adjustments.

2. **Optimization:** By tracking KPIs, you can identify areas for improvement and optimize your marketing strategies to achieve better results.

3. **Resource allocation:** Understanding the performance of your marketing channels helps you allocate resources more effectively, focusing on the strategies that generate the highest ROI.

4. **Goal-setting:** Establishing and tracking KPIs enables you to set realistic marketing goals and measure progress towards achieving them.

Common Marketing KPIs

Some common KPIs to consider tracking for various marketing channels include:

1. **Website:** Website traffic, bounce rate, average session duration, conversion rate, and goal completions.

2. **Social media:** Follower growth, engagement rate, reach, impressions, and conversions.

3. **Email marketing:** Open rate, click-through rate, conversion rate, unsubscribe rate, and list growth.

4. **SEO:** Organic search traffic, keyword rankings, click-through rate, and conversions.

5. **PPC advertising:** Click-through rate, cost per click, conversion rate, and return on ad spend.

6. **Content marketing:** Page views, time on page, social shares, and lead generation.

7. **Event marketing:** Attendance, leads generated, conversion rate, and overall event satisfaction.

Tips for Effective Marketing Measurement

To effectively measure your marketing success, consider the following tips:

1. **Select relevant KPIs:** Choose KPIs that align with your marketing objectives and provide meaningful insights into your campaign performance.

2. **Establish benchmarks:** Determine baseline metrics for each KPI to help you evaluate progress and success over time.

3. **Utilize analytics tools:** Leverage tools like Google Analytics, social media analytics, and email marketing platforms to track your KPIs and gather insights.

4. **Monitor and adjust:** Regularly review your KPIs and analytics data to identify trends, areas for improvement, and opportunities for optimization.

5. **Report and communicate:** Share your marketing performance data with relevant stakeholders, such as team members or business partners, to ensure alignment and support informed decision-making.

By effectively measuring your marketing success through analytics and KPIs, you can make data-driven decisions, optimize your strategies, and achieve better results for your small business. In the following chapters, we'll explore more marketing strategies and channels to help you create well-rounded advertising campaigns that achieve your business goals.

Chapter 16:
Creating an Integrated Marketing Plan: Combining Traditional and Digital Strategies

An integrated marketing plan combines traditional marketing methods, such as radio advertising, with digital strategies to create a cohesive, multi-channel campaign that effectively engages your target audience. In this chapter, we'll discuss the benefits of integrated marketing and provide tips for developing a successful integrated marketing plan.

Benefits of Integrated Marketing

1. **Consistent messaging:** Combining traditional and digital strategies ensures your brand message is consistent across all channels, reinforcing your brand identity and increasing recognition.

2. **Expanded reach:** By leveraging multiple marketing channels, you can reach a broader audience and increase the likelihood of engaging potential customers.

3. **Increased engagement:** A well-coordinated integrated marketing plan can create a seamless customer experience, encouraging higher engagement and ultimately driving conversions.

4. **Improved ROI:** Integrated marketing allows you to optimize your marketing budget by allocating resources more effectively and maximizing the impact of each channel.

Tips for Developing a Successful Integrated Marketing Plan

1. **Set clear objectives:** Define your marketing goals, such as increasing brand awareness, generating leads, or boosting sales. These objectives will guide your integrated marketing plan and help you measure its success.

2. **Identify your target audience:** Understand your ideal customer's demographics, preferences, and pain points to create targeted and relevant marketing messages.

3. **Choose the right channels:** Select a mix of traditional and digital marketing channels that align with your target audience and objectives. For example, radio advertising can be combined with social media, content marketing, and email campaigns.

4. **Create consistent messaging:** Develop a unified brand message that resonates with your target audience and can be adapted for each marketing channel.

5. **Develop a coordinated campaign:** Plan and schedule your marketing activities across all channels to ensure a cohesive and coordinated customer experience.

6. **Measure and optimize:** Track the performance of your integrated marketing plan using analytics and KPIs, making adjustments as needed to improve results and maximize ROI.

Example: Coordinated Radio and Digital Marketing Campaign

To create an effective integrated marketing campaign that combines radio and digital strategies, consider the following steps:

1. **Develop a compelling radio ad:** Create a radio advertisement that captures your brand message, highlights your product or service, and includes a clear call-to-action.

2. **Extend the message online:** Use your website, social media, and email marketing to expand upon the message from your radio ad, providing additional information and opportunities for engagement.

3. **Leverage social media:** Share your radio ad on social media platforms, encouraging followers to engage with your content and share it within their networks.

4. **Track and measure results:** Monitor the performance of both your radio and digital marketing efforts, analyzing data such as website traffic, social media engagement, and lead generation to optimize your integrated campaign.

By creating an integrated marketing plan that combines traditional and digital strategies, you can effectively engage your target audience, reinforce your brand message, and drive results for your small business. In the following chapters, we'll explore more marketing strategies and channels to help you create well-rounded advertising campaigns that achieve your business goals.

Chapter 17: Growth Hacking Techniques for Small Businesses

Growth hacking is a marketing approach that focuses on rapid, cost-effective strategies to achieve significant growth in a short period. For small businesses with limited resources, growth hacking can be an effective way to scale quickly and gain a competitive advantage. In this chapter, we'll discuss some growth hacking techniques that small businesses can implement to drive rapid growth.

Growth Hacking Techniques

1. **Leverage existing networks:** Utilize your personal and professional networks to promote your business, reach new customers, and generate referrals. Encourage satisfied customers to share their experiences within their own networks.
2. **Offer incentives:** Create referral programs, discounts, or exclusive offers to encourage customers to promote your business and bring in new clients. This not only increases customer acquisition but also helps with customer retention.
3. **Create viral content:** Develop engaging, shareable content that resonates with your target audience. This could include blog posts, infographics, videos, or social media posts that can potentially go viral and generate significant organic reach.
4. **Optimize conversion rates:** Continuously test and optimize your website, landing pages, and marketing materials to increase conversion rates. Focus on improving user experience, simplifying the sales funnel, and addressing potential customer objections.
5. **Collaborate with influencers:** Partner with influencers in your industry to expand your reach and tap into their established audience. Collaborate on content, promotions, or events to create buzz and drive growth.
6. **Automate processes:** Automate repetitive tasks, such as social media posting, email marketing, or lead nurturing, using available tools and software. This frees up time and resources, allowing you to focus on growth-driving activities.
7. **Leverage data:** Gather and analyze data from your marketing efforts to make data-driven decisions, identify areas for improvement, and optimize your strategies for maximum results.
8. **Experiment and iterate:** Embrace a growth hacking mindset by continuously testing new ideas, learning from failures, and iterating on successful strategies. Be agile and adaptable, responding to market changes and customer feedback.

Tips for Implementing Growth Hacking Techniques

1. **Set clear goals:** Define your growth objectives and identify the metrics you'll use to measure success.

2. **Prioritize your efforts:** Focus on the growth hacking techniques that are most likely to generate the highest ROI for your specific business and target audience.

3. **Allocate resources wisely:** Use your limited resources strategically, prioritizing cost-effective strategies and automating processes where possible.

4. **Monitor and analyze results:** Regularly review your growth hacking efforts, analyzing data to identify successes, areas for improvement, and opportunities for optimization.

By implementing growth hacking techniques, small businesses can rapidly scale their operations, attract new customers, and gain a competitive edge in the market. In the following chapters, we'll explore more marketing strategies and channels to help you create well-rounded advertising campaigns that achieve your business goals.

Chapter 18:
The Future of Advertising and Marketing: Trends to Watch

As technology continues to evolve, the advertising and marketing landscape is constantly changing. Staying ahead of the curve and understanding emerging trends can help businesses adapt their strategies and maintain a competitive edge. In this chapter, we'll discuss some key trends to watch in the future of advertising and marketing.

Emerging Trends in Advertising and Marketing

1. **Artificial Intelligence (AI):** AI-driven technologies are becoming increasingly sophisticated and are poised to revolutionize the advertising and marketing industry. With applications such as chatbots, personalized content, and predictive analytics, AI can improve customer experiences, streamline processes, and optimize marketing efforts.

2. **Voice Search Optimization:** As voice-activated devices like smart speakers and virtual assistants become more prevalent, optimizing your content for voice search will be crucial for maintaining visibility and reaching your target audience.

3. **Augmented Reality (AR) and Virtual Reality (VR):** AR and VR technologies offer immersive experiences that can engage customers, enhance product visualization, and create memorable brand interactions. Incorporating these technologies into your marketing strategies can help you stand out from the competition.

4. **Video Content:** Video content continues to grow in popularity, with platforms such as YouTube, TikTok, and Instagram driving demand for engaging, shareable videos. Investing in video production and incorporating video content into your marketing mix can help you capture your audience's attention and boost engagement.

5. **Omnichannel Marketing:** Delivering a seamless, consistent experience across multiple touchpoints is becoming increasingly important in today's connected world. An omnichannel marketing approach ensures a cohesive customer journey, regardless of the channel or device they use to interact with your brand.

6. **Data Privacy and Security:** As data privacy regulations like GDPR and CCPA become more prominent, businesses must prioritize data protection and transparency in their marketing efforts. Ensuring compliance with these regulations and building trust with your customers will be essential for success.

7. **Sustainable and Ethical Marketing:** Consumers are increasingly concerned about the environmental and social impact of their purchasing decisions. Incorporating sustainability and ethical practices into your marketing strategy can help you appeal to a growing segment of conscious consumers.

Preparing for the Future of Advertising and Marketing

To stay ahead in the ever-evolving marketing landscape, consider the following tips:

1. **Stay informed:** Regularly research industry news, emerging technologies, and marketing trends to stay up-to-date on developments that could impact your business.

2. **Invest in innovation:** Allocate resources to test and implement new technologies and strategies that align with your business goals and target audience.

3. **Embrace agility:** Be prepared to adapt your marketing strategies quickly in response to changing consumer preferences, technological advancements, and market conditions.

4. **Focus on customer experience:** Prioritize delivering exceptional customer experiences across all marketing channels, leveraging emerging technologies to enhance personalization and engagement.

By keeping an eye on emerging trends and adapting your marketing strategies accordingly, you can ensure your business remains competitive and well-positioned for future success in the ever-changing advertising landscape. In the following chapters, we'll explore various marketing strategies and channels to help you create well-rounded advertising campaigns that achieve your business goals.

Chapter 19: Case Studies of Successful Small Business Marketing Campaigns

Learning from the success of others can provide valuable insights and inspiration for your own marketing efforts. In this chapter, we'll explore several case studies of small businesses that have implemented successful marketing campaigns.

Case Study 1: Dollar Shave Club - Viral Video Launch

Dollar Shave Club, a subscription-based razor company, gained immense popularity in 2012 after releasing a low-budget, humorous video featuring their CEO, Michael Dubin. The video went viral, garnering millions of views and catapulting the brand into the spotlight.

Key Takeaways:
- Create engaging, shareable content that resonates with your target audience.
- Inject humor and personality into your marketing to make your brand memorable.
- Leverage the power of social media and video content to reach a wider audience.

Case Study 2: Death Wish Coffee - Super Bowl Ad Win

Death Wish Coffee, a small coffee roastery, won a contest in 2016 that awarded them a free 30-second commercial during the Super Bowl. The ad highlighted their strong, bold coffee and unique branding, resulting in a significant increase in sales and brand recognition.

Key Takeaways:

- Take advantage of contests and promotional opportunities to gain exposure.
- Develop a unique selling proposition (USP) that sets your brand apart from competitors.
- Use high-profile advertising opportunities to showcase your brand's personality and product offerings.

Case Study 3: GoldieBlox - Empowering Girls Through Content Marketing

GoldieBlox, a toy company focused on encouraging girls to pursue STEM fields, launched a series of content marketing campaigns featuring empowering messages and stories. By creating engaging blog posts, videos, and social media content, they successfully connected with their target audience and generated buzz around their brand.

Key Takeaways:

- Align your marketing messages with your brand's values and mission.
- Create content that resonates with your target audience's interests and aspirations.
- Utilize various content formats (e.g., blog posts, videos, social media) to reach and engage your audience.

Case Study 4: Beardbrand - Building a Community Through Social Media

Beardbrand, a men's grooming company, successfully leveraged social media to build a loyal community around their brand. By sharing educational content, engaging with followers, and showcasing real customers' stories, they cultivated a strong online presence and attracted a dedicated fan base.

Key Takeaways:

- Focus on building genuine connections with your audience through social media.
- Share valuable, informative content that addresses your target audience's needs and interests.
- Encourage user-generated content and showcase real customer experiences to foster trust and authenticity.

By studying these successful small business marketing campaigns, you can gather insights and inspiration to develop your own marketing strategies. Remember to focus on engaging and resonating with your target audience, leveraging various marketing channels, and continuously adapting and optimizing your efforts for maximum impact. In the following chapters, we'll explore more marketing strategies and channels to help you create well-rounded advertising campaigns that achieve your business goals.

Chapter 20: Final Thoughts

Throughout this guide, we've explored various marketing strategies, channels, and trends to help you create well-rounded advertising campaigns that achieve your business goals. As a small business owner, it's essential to stay informed about the ever-evolving marketing landscape and continuously adapt your strategies to remain competitive.

Here are some final thoughts to consider as you embark on your marketing journey:

1.   **Know your audience:** Understanding your target audience's needs, preferences, and pain points is the foundation of any successful marketing campaign. Invest time in researching and defining your ideal customer to create targeted, relevant marketing messages.

2.   **Set clear objectives:** Establish specific, measurable, achievable, relevant, and time-bound (SMART) goals for your marketing efforts. These objectives will guide your strategies and help you measure their success.

3.   **Embrace an integrated approach:** Utilize a mix of traditional and digital marketing channels to create a cohesive, multi-channel campaign that effectively engages your target audience.

4.   **Focus on customer experience:** Prioritize delivering exceptional customer experiences across all marketing touchpoints. This includes providing personalized content, seamless interactions, and responsive customer support.

5.   **Test, analyze, and optimize:** Regularly review your marketing performance using analytics and key performance indicators (KPIs). Use these insights to make data-driven decisions, optimize your strategies, and improve your results.

6.   **Stay agile:** Be prepared to adapt your marketing strategies in response to changing consumer preferences, technological advancements, and market conditions. Embrace a growth mindset and continuously iterate on your marketing efforts.

7.   **Invest in innovation:** Allocate resources to test and implement new technologies and strategies that align with your business goals and target audience. Staying ahead of the curve can give you a competitive edge in the market.

By keeping these principles in mind and continually refining your marketing strategies, you can effectively engage your target audience, build brand awareness, and drive growth for your small business. Remember that marketing is an ongoing process, and success comes from a persistent, adaptable approach that evolves with your business and market landscape. Good luck on your marketing journey!
If you're looking for my help, reach out. My passion is helping small business owners succeed. I can help you grow your business. Find me through my free marketing help website FreeMarketingHelp.org Follow me on Instagram, Twitter and Tiktok.

Keith
@graywaterops
Small business owner, Senior Media Consultant
Artist, Creative Thinker & Writer

www.ingramcontent.com/pod-product-compliance
Lightning Source LLC
Chambersburg PA
CBHW051924210526

45473CB00006B/2131